About the author

Alexandre Dumas was born in France in 1802. His father – a disgraced Bonapartist general – died while he was still a child, but his mother's tales of his bravery during the Napoleonic wars inspired the young Alexandre to write some of the best-loved adventure stories the world has known.

At the age of 22, Dumas left home and travelled to Paris where he found fame as a playwright and novelist. While his plays continued to find success, after a few years Dumas turned his attention to novels, which he astutely serialised for publication in literature-hungry magazines. Such a strategy provided Dumas with a generous income – a necessity, given his tendency to live extravagantly and consistently spend more than he earned.

Dumas compiled an enormous body of work over the course of his life. His best-loved works are his epic adventures, such as *The Three Musketeers* and *The Count of Monte Cristo*. He died in 1870 in Puys, and in 2002, in honour of his enduring legacy, his remains were moved to the Pantheon in Paris and interred alongside other French luminaries.

CHARACTERS

EDMOND DANTÈS

COUNT OF MONTE CRISTO

ABBÉ BUSONI

ABBÉ FARIA

MERCÉDÈS

HAIDÉE

VILLEFORT

FERNAND

DANGLARS

CADEROUSSE

THE COUNT OF MONTE CRISTO

ALEXANDRE DUMAS

THE COUNT OF MONTE CRISTO

Alexandre Dumas

Sitting around the Campfire, telling the story, were:

WORDSMITH
R JAY NUDDS

EDITOR
ADITI RAY

ILLUSTRATOR
SANKHA BANERJEE

COLOURIST
ANIL C K

DESKTOP PUBLISHING
BHAVNATH CHAUDHARY

COVER ART
SANKHA BANERJEE & ANIL C K

CAMPFIRE®

www.campfire.co.in

Published by Kalyani Navyug Media Pvt Ltd
101 C, Shiv House, Hari Nagar Ashram, New Delhi 110014, India

ISBN: 978-93-80028-01-9

Printed in India

When Alexandre Dumas set out to write *The Count of Monte Cristo*, his intention was to reconstruct French history through a series of novels and teach the French people about their history and heritage. Although *The Count of Monte Cristo* does not follow the facts exactly, elements of reality woven into the text have a profound effect on the characters and their actions. Penned in 1844, this classic novel looks back on a tumultuous time for French politics at the turn of the nineteenth century.

Set between 1815 and 1838, *The Count of Monte Cristo* sees the control of France change hands on more than one occasion. To understand the gravity of the social upheaval experienced at this time, we need to go back further in the history of France to the dawn of the French Revolution that ultimately brought Napoléon Bonaparte to power.

By 1789 the French people had become so angry with the monarchy that they revolted. Four years later, in 1793, King Louis XVI was executed, and France belonged to the people. But without organised rule, a year of confusion known as the Reign of Terror followed, claiming between 16,000 and 40,000 lives in 1794.

In the years that followed, bloody wars led to the French army taking control of the Italian peninsula and parts of Germany – achievements that exceeded those of any previous French government. The 'Directory' then assumed control of the state, until it was replaced by the 'Consulate', headed by Napoléon Bonaparte, who proclaimed himself 'Emperor'.

Napoléon's reign, defined by his insatiable thirst for power, was brought to a shuddering halt in 1814, when opposing European powers restored the fallen monarchy by force.

It is during this period that *The Count of Monte Cristo* begins. The people of France were divided: some welcomed the king's return and worked hard at establishing his new rule, but many still supported Napoléon. Bonapartists became outlaws; having sympathy for the Emperor's cause was a crime punishable by death or exile. So many went underground, kept their mouths shut, or lied about their loyalties to the king in order to survive.

But in 1815, one month after our tale begins, Napoléon returned to power, storming Paris and regaining control of the state. His second stint in charge lasted only 100 days, before the opposing armies of Europe descended and removed him for good in the Battle of Waterloo.

Many characters in *The Count of Monte Cristo* are motivated by their political allegiances, and they all deal with this burden in different ways.

Poor Edmond Dantès, the hero of our tale, appears to have no feelings on the subject and, perhaps due to his youth, is ignorant of the severe consequences of finding oneself on the 'wrong' side. Unluckily, he becomes entangled with political wranglings far beyond his understanding.

The shift between King and Emperor, and the effect their rule has on the characters in this epic adventure, is essential to our understanding of the story. Given below is a timeline of the flip-flopping control of France:

1789 – 1792
The French Revolution begins and the French First Republic is founded

1793
King Louis XVI is executed and the monarchy deposed

1793 – 1794
The Reign of Terror

1795 – 1799
The Directory takes control of the French First Republic

1799 – 1804
The Consulate and Napoléon take control of the French First Republic

1805 – 1814
The French First Republic becomes the French First Empire under Napoléon

1814 (11th April)
The French monarchy is restored with help from other European powers

1815 (24th February)
The Count of Monte Cristo begins, and Edmond Dantès returns to Marseilles

1815 (25th February)
Edmond Dantès is imprisoned in the Château d'If for being a Bonapartist agent

1815 (20th March – 7th July)
Napoléon returns to power for 100 days

1815 (7th July)
Napoléon is defeated in the Battle of Waterloo, the French monarchy is restored, and Dantès remains in prison

On 24th February 1815, the *Pharaon* returned to Marseilles after a three-month voyage that had claimed the life of its captain and seen first mate Edmond Dantès take the helm.

During the *Pharaon's* absence, France had undergone a radical political change: Emperor Napoléon had been deposed and was in hiding, but was already plotting his return to power.

Those who supported him were being hunted down and jailed or executed by the king's agents. And so it was a troubled world to which Dantès and his crew returned.

In the family home, Old Dantès was tending to his nasturtiums, as he had done every day since his beloved son set sail...

...sitting by the window in the hope that he might see the face of his only child approach.

He could barely afford to eat, nor could he sleep for worrying over Edmond's safe return. Too often, ships were lost at sea and their crew forgotten.

Every sound on the stair set the old man's heart racing, such was the love shared by father and son.

CCRRREI

For three long months, he waited and prayed, until the day...

KNOCK
KNOCK

...his prayers were answered.

Father!

Edmond! Oh, praise the Lord, it is you!

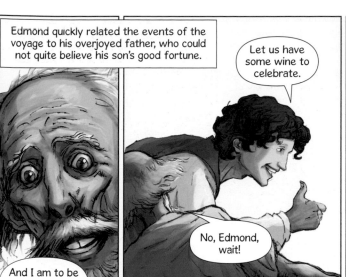

Edmond quickly related the events of the voyage to his overjoyed father, who could not quite believe his son's good fortune.

And I am to be made Captain of the *Pharaon*!

Let us have some wine to celebrate.

No, Edmond, wait!

Father, where is the wine... where is all your food?

There is no wine... and not much in the way of food. I have been struck down by poverty, Edmond. I owe a great deal of money to our neighbour, Caderousse.

I cannot believe he has let you suffer like this in my absence!

Here, take my wages and pay off your debts.

At that moment, Caderousse appeared at the door.

Ah, Edmond, how nice it is to see you...

...and your gold!

Take what you're owed, Caderousse, but after that I want you to leave my father alone. I must go now, there is someone I am desperate to see.

Dantès headed to the village of the Catalans, home to his betrothed, the beautiful Mercédès.

But in Dantès's absence, a rival for her love had wormed his way into her life: her cousin Fernand, a jealous and impatient man.

Why can you not see how much I love you, Mercédès? Leave him and marry me instead!

Fernand, you are a dear friend – almost like a brother to me. But my heart belongs to Edmond. I know he will come back for me, and then I will be his wife!

You are mad! He is married to the sea and is nothing but a common sailor!

I will take that chance for true love.

But he can never provide for you in the way I--

Mercédès!

Mercédès! Oh, how I have missed you!

And I you!

Darling, you remember my cousin, Fernand? He has taken care of me while you have been away.

I am in your debt, Fernand. A friend of Mercédès is a friend of mine.

I... I must go.

Unable to stand the pain of seeing the lovers reunited, Fernand fled from Mercédès's home.

As Fernand walked away dejected, he was spotted by his old friends, Danglars and Caderousse...

Hello there, Fernand! What's the hurry?

Take a seat, friend, and tell us your troubles.

Reluctantly, Fernand joined the pair.

What on earth's the matter? You look like you have seen a ghost!

I might as well have. Edmond Dantès has returned, and has claimed Mercédès!

Well, I'll drink to that – hic – to Edmond! A fine fellow!

Will you shut up – you're drunk!

I am nn... o... t drunk! To Dantès – a prince among men!

Oh God, he is right! There is no way I will be able to win Mercédès's heart while he is around.

Danglars wants him gone too – hic – says young Edmond stole his ship.

Shut your mouth, Caderousse. You are too drunk to think... but maybe...

Maybe what?

Maybe our drunken friend has struck upon the answer. Neither of us can get what we want while Edmond is around.

I want the Pharaon, and you want Mercédès. If Edmond were to... disappear... our paths would be cleared.

Would you have us kill him!?

Nothing so... messy. I have a plan!

13

Have some more wine and hold your tongue, there's a good man.

Why are you two talking like this? Edmond is a fine fellow, I say! He deserves everything he's got. Let him be.

What do you know, Danglars? How can we get rid of him?

I overheard Captain Leclère giving Edmond instructions to deliver a letter in Paris – a letter addressed to a supporter of the Emperor*.

You mean Edmond is in possession of this letter?! But that is treason! Does he know what he holds?

*Napoléon Bonaparte

He is too trusting to doubt Leclère. It is just a thought, but if I were to take a piece of paper...

...and using my left hand, write a message to the king's men in Marseilles, informing them of Edmond's role as a Bonapartist agent... well, the boy would be arrested immediately.

What a wicked notion, Danglars – I hope you are joking!

Of course I am, my friend. Look, I shall dispose of the letter at once.

True to his word, Danglars crumpled up the incriminating letter and threw it at Fernand's feet, making sure to give the lovesick young man a knowing look...

...at which Fernand picked up the letter.

Oh look, here comes the happy couple now!

This letter... I wonder...

Hello there!

Edmond, how good to see you looking so well! Sorry about leaving your father in such a state. Money can divide the closest of friends, you know.

Rest easy, Caderousse, he is safe and well now. I see no reason to bear a grudge.

Besides, my heart is filled with nothing but happiness – Mercédès has agreed to be my wife!

Your wife?!

Indeed! We are to marry tomorrow. And all of you are invited to the celebration.

Tomorrow?

Oh God, I must stop this! She has to be mine!

A thousand congratulations, Edmond! You two make a lovely couple!

Come now, Caderousse, let us go home. You have had plenty of wine. Leave some for our friend, Fernand.

Congratulations, Edmond. What a day it must be for you!

Congra – hic – tula – hic...

We, too, should take our leave. There is much to arrange for tomorrow!

Looking back, Danglars noticed the young Catalan deep in thought.

And so it begins...

The next day, guests gathered for the wedding of Dantès and Mercédès. Those present basked in the contentment and happiness that radiated from the betrothed couple. All but Fernand...

Damn it, Caderousse, are you drunk already? You can hardly stand straight!

I'm watching Fernand. Does he not look strange to you? He keeps fidgeting and looking out of the window in the direction of Marseilles.

Fernand could hardly keep his eyes from the road to Marseilles, much less enjoy the party. Danglars watched the Catalan with interest, daring to hope his evil scheme might yet ruin Dantès's ambitions.

Danglars! Caderousse! How good of you to come!

We would not miss it for the world, Edmond!

Yes, it promises to be quite a show!

At that moment, the sound of hurried footsteps approached the party.

It sounds like we may have to welcome more guests!

Open up in the name of the king!

BOOM BOOM

What on earth...

CRACK!

Which one among you is Edmond Dantès?

I am.

Sir, I have a warrant for your arrest. You must come with me.

Oh Edmond, what is all this?! That too on our wedding day!

Don't worry, my love. It's no doubt some business with the *Pharaon's* cargo — it is quite common.

I will be back in a couple of hours. Take care of the guests. I will see you soon.

Meanwhile, in the centre of Marseilles, Gérard de Villefort, Deputy Prosecutor to the king, was throwing a party to mark his own marriage to Renée de Saint-Méran.

Although he celebrated the same occasion as the unfortunate Dantès, his guests could not have been more different from the rough and ready rabble attending Edmond's feast.

Seated around the table were the flowers of Marseilles: magistrates loyal to the king; officers who had deserted Napoléon and fought instead for their monarch; and the younger generation of France who had been brought up to hate the usurped Emperor.

I said do you agree, Monsieur de Villefort?

And it was inevitable that the conversation should turn to the fate of the deposed and his legacy. However, as one might expect of a man celebrating his wedding, Villefort's mind was elsewhere, and it was with great effort that Marquise de Saint-Méran, his mother-in-law, earned his attention.

I beg your pardon, madame, but I was not really following the conversation.

What I said was that the Bonapartists did not have the sincerity, enthusiasm, or devotion that we Royalists have.

True, but Napoléon was worshipped like a god.

Ha! Once, maybe! But he who ruled France governs nothing now but the petty Island of Elba.

He was once viewed as the very personification of equality. I would wager Napoléon retains many covert supporters.

You are talking like a revolutionary yourself!

But then, you *are* the son of a loyal Bonapartist.

Yes, my father supported the Emperor, but he was tried and very nearly lost his head.

Unlike *my* father who died for his principles. *Yours* was quick to join the new government. I believe they call him *Senator* Noirtier these days?

Mother, it was agreed that these memories would be laid aside. Gérard shares none of his father's loyalties.

Renée is right. I have denounced my heritage entirely and intend to be firm in my post as Prosecutor to the king – no traitor will slip through my grasp.

At that moment, a messenger interrupted the party...

Sir, you are required at once to deal with an urgent matter.

When Villefort arrived at his office in Marseilles, he was met by a much vexed Monsieur Morrel, who had left Dantès's feast in the hope of saving his friend.

Monsieur de Villefort?

Good evening, monsieur. What can I do for you?

My name is Morrel, sir. I have come with regard to the arrest of one of my men, Edmond Dantès.

Although they had never met, Villefort knew all about Morrel and his sympathies with the Emperor. He had studied the notes on Dantès's case on the way to his office, and was keen to hear what the old ship owner had to say.

Is he a good man, this Dantès fellow?

The finest! Why, he is the most estimable of all my crew, and a great friend.

Be that as it may, Morrel. As you well know from your own... dealings... a man may be estimable in his private life, and a great traitor in political terms.

I know you must take issue with my loyalties, sir, but I can assure you that Dantès is no traitor. He is just an innocent boy!

Very well, Morrel, I will interview him with an open mind. If he is as innocent as you say he is, he will be released within the hour. Good day.

Morrel left the office, and Dantès was brought in.

Edmond Dantès?

Yes, sir.

Please sit down, Monsieur Dantès, and tell me why I have been called away from my wedding party.

Well, sir, the truth is I am not quite sure. I was arrested and brought here because I possess a letter given to me by a friend of the late Captain Leclère.

It would seem I am caught up in some dark business, but I swear to you I know not what it is.

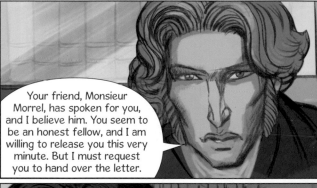

Your friend, Monsieur Morrel, has spoken for you, and I believe him. You seem to be an honest fellow, and I am willing to release you this very minute. But I must request you to hand over the letter.

The letter must be with you, sir. I heard the guards confiscated it along with other papers from my house.

Oh yes... your papers are here in this packet... this must be it.

Monsieur Noirtier, Rue Coq-Héron, Paris.

Noirtier... my father!

Where did you say you got this letter?

From Marshal Bertrand on the Island of Elba. I was acting under the instruction of the late Captain Leclère. I have no idea what the letter contains.

He seems to be telling the truth, but what if he's lying? What if he knows the contents of this letter? There is no doubt that it is a message from the Emperor to my father. If this gets out, I will be ruined!

I must get rid of Dantès... but, oh God, what if he's innocent?

Can I imprison an innocent man to save my own skin?

I have worked too hard for this... I have... no choice...

Very well, Dantès, you will be escorted to the Palais de Justice by my guards, where you shall await your release papers.

Then you believe me?

I do, Dantès... I do... now go.

While Dantès was being taken to the Palais de Justice, Villefort plotted how best to cover himself. He destroyed the letter addressed to his father, and wrote a letter to the king detailing his discovery and single-handed capture of the violent Bonapartist... Edmond Dantès!

At the Palais de Justice, Dantès found himself thrown in a cell where he waited for the arrival of his release papers.

I don't fancy life behind bars. Not when the sea calls to me so.

Eventually, after night had fallen, Dantès was collected by two royal guards and escorted to a coach.

Get in!

Dantès did as he was told, grateful to be out of jail.

Where are we going?

But no answer came from the guards. The coach trundled on until it came to a stop.

Bewildered, Dantès found himself bundled into a small boat.

Where are we going?!

To the Château d'If, scum. Now shut your mouth.

The Château d'If! NO!

Where are we going?

Château d'If, the most feared prison in all of France. No man had ever escaped its sheer walls, around which rose a terrifying maw of jagged rocks, lapped at the edges by the unceasing squall of the sea.

Terrified by the prospect, Dantès tried to dive overboard...

HEY YOU!

...but was grabbed by the burly guards and slammed against the floor of the boat.

Try that again, and you won't see the sun rise, boy!

Dantès broke down. His life, his Mercédès, had been cruelly torn from him at the moment of his greatest happiness.

Soon the silhouette of the Château d'If loomed in the moonlight.

I wish the guard had pulled the trigger! God, save me from this hell!

He was thrown into a cell and given a new name: Prisoner 34.

His life as Edmond Dantès was, barring a miracle, over.

LET ME GO! I AM INNOCENT! I DEMAND TO SEE THE GOVERNOR!

But no one responded to Dantès's cry for help.

Later, when the jailer came to check on him, Dantès made a desperate bid for freedom.

Not so fast, No. 34.

Let me go, I'm innocent!

Oh, ho, ho, another mad one! We've got one just like you in the dungeon – Abbé Faria, he calls himself – who tries to buy his freedom with imaginary treasure.

Crazy fool! There is no way out of here, No. 34. This is the end of the road.

And so it was that for the next year, Edmond Dantès was left to rot in his cell.

Villefort delivered his findings to the king, asserting that Dantès was a dangerous supporter of Napoléon and unfit for release.

Villefort's father, Noirtier, proclaimed that the Emperor would return, and soon after, Napoléon stormed Paris and took control of France again.

Monsieur Morrel sought an audience with the Emperor and pleaded for Dantès to be set free. He claimed that Dantès was indeed a long-time supporter and, for a while, it looked as if he might be successful.

But fate played a cruel trick on the well-meaning Morrel, for Napoléon's reign lasted but a few months, and with the king reinstated, the ship owner's testimony that Dantès had been a traitor was used to keep him in the Château d'If.

Old Dantès and Mercédès were distraught that nothing could be done. Despite the best efforts of his friends, Dantès was doomed to die within the impregnable walls of the island fortress.

Forever imprisoned, forever forgotten by the outside world.

In March 1816, one year after entering the Château d'If, Dantès was visited by the new governor.

This is Prisoner No. 34, sir. He's a mad one – tried to kill me once.

Look alive, will you? The governor's come to inspect the cells!

Oh, sir, thank God you have come! Perhaps you will look into my case and see me freed. I am innocent, I swear it!

Yes, prisoners always do. I seem to remember your case, No. 34. Were you not examined by the eminent prosecutor, Gérard de Villefort?

Indeed I was, sir, and I beg of you to talk to him. You can trust his word, sir – he believes I am innocent!

Very well, No. 34, I will look over his notes. Good day to you.

Dantès was left with a glimmer of hope.

Metres of solid rock separated Dantès's cell from that of his neighbour, Prisoner No. 27 – Abbé Faria.

If you thought No. 34 was mad, wait until you meet our abbé.

He talks a lot of gibberish, sir. Try not to pay much attention to what he says.

Governor! Have you come to release me?

I will reward you handsomely if you set me free!

I know of a great treasure hoard and will share it with you if you let me go... I can make you a wealthy man!

Get back, you wretch! You see sir, he is mad! He will never leave the Château d'If.

You will die within these walls, No. 27. Mark my words!

The governor made his way out of the dungeon, but he did not feel at ease as he left.

No. 34 seems so genuine, so innocent, and No. 27 is nothing but a poor old man who wants his freedom. Neither seems dangerous.

Although the governor held out little hope for Dantès, he was, if nothing else, an honest man, and he looked into No. 34's case.

The trusting Dantès had assured the governor that the conniving Villefort could be believed, and so the governor requested the report of the king's prosecutor.

O, the poor man...

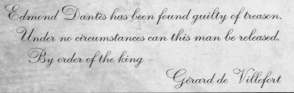

Edmond Dantès has been found guilty of treason. Under no circumstances can this man be released. By order of the king –

Gérard de Villefort

There was no hope.

As the years rolled by, Dantès kept track of the time with a sharp stone that had broken away from the wall.

But soon days and nights ceased to mean anything, and he lost count.

The years passed, and he resolved to end his suffering by starving himself to death.

The end was near.

There is... nothing... left...

SCRAPE
SCRAPE
SCRAPE
SCRAPE

At the moment of his greatest despair, a noise coming from under the floor threw the arms of hope around Dantès's wretched frame...

There's someone under the floor!

Hello, hello? Can you hear me?

To Dantès's astonishment, a flagstone at his feet began to shift.

Emerging from beneath was Abbé Faria!

Although they had never met before, their shared situation bonded them in an instant.

No. 34, is it? I've heard them call your number.

My friends call me... *called* me Edmond Dantès. And you are Abbé Faria. Are you as mad as they say?

I must be! My tunnel was supposed to lead to the outer walls, but now I find myself in another cell.

Come with me, Edmond. My tunnel needs to be made more secure, and you can help!

Dantès was glad of the exercise, but gladder still of a friend. Together they completed the abbé's secret passage, taking care not to disturb the guards with their midnight labours.

Using the tunnel, Dantès took to visiting the old man every night once the guards had gone to sleep.

The abbé would tell Dantès tales of a great treasure hoard he knew to be hidden on the Island of Monte Cristo.

It can make you wealthy beyond your imagination!

Maybe there is some truth in what he is saying.

At first Dantès disbelieved him, but the abbé seemed so sincere, the young man could not help but dream.

The abbé would keep close track of the date, and Dantès was surprised to learn that almost seven years had passed since his imprisonment. The boy of nineteen was now a man of twenty-six!

...and you say you have no idea who put you here?

I trusted all my friends... why would anyone betray me?

Jealousy is a powerful emotion, Edmond... you must think! Who had most to gain from your absence?

Over the following days, Abbé Faria helped Dantès deduce the identity of his betrayers.

It was clear now that Danglars's desire to captain the *Pharaon* and Fernand's desperation to marry Mercédès had driven them to commit the most heinous of crimes. But Dantès still needed proof.

They proved a fine pair: the abbé was a wise man and appeared perfectly sane to Dantès, whose enquiring mind excited the old man.

The abbé took it upon himself to educate the rough but keen sailor in the hope that he might become a fine, intelligent man worthy of sharing the treasure and capable of avenging his betrayal, should they escape.

Over the following years, Dantès became an expert in the science and art of poison...

...the master of many languages and cultures...

...an intriguing gentleman and conversationalist...

...and a gifted financier with a vast knowledge of money and how it could be used.

33

Bravo, Edmond, bravo! You are truly magnificent! Never in all my years at the monastery was I blessed with such a fine pupil. You--

AARRRGGHHH

The abbé had warned Dantès that he had suffered cataleptic fits in the past. He had prepared a special medicine to ease the pain and had told his young protégé where it was hidden, should he be struck down by another attack.

Here, my friend, drink this.

There... do you feel better now?

I will survive this time, but I am dying, my boy. It is only a matter of time.

Dantès put his old friend to bed and returned to his cell. He lay awake the rest of the night, hoping for the recovery of his sole confidant.

Without the abbé he would be doomed to live and die alone.

The next night, Dantès was woken up by an awful sound.

The abbé is having another fit!

GAAAA

He rushed through the passage to find his friend at death's door...

Abbé, are you alright?

AAAAA!

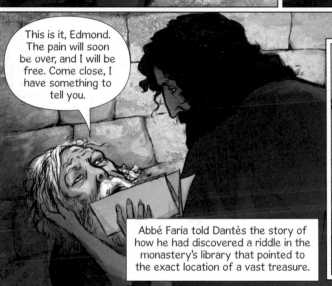

This is it, Edmond. The pain will soon be over, and I will be free. Come close, I have something to tell you.

Abbé Faria told Dantès the story of how he had discovered a riddle in the monastery's library that pointed to the exact location of a vast treasure.

Here, take this. It will lead you to the treasure.

You have been like a son to me, Edmond. You have brought a great deal of comfort to an old and lonely man. The treasure is my gift to you. Use it and live well. Goodbye, Edmond. Be free.

And then, in the dark seclusion of his cell, the kind Abbé Faria breathed his last.

The abbé's fit had woken the guards.

Come on, let's get the other things needed to dispose of this body.

Maybe I could...

Without a sound, Dantès leapt out of the tunnel – he had to act fast!

He dragged the abbé's body through the tunnel and into his own cell, where he covered his dead friend with a blanket.

He hurried back into the abbé's cell, slipped into the empty body bag, sewed it up from the inside...

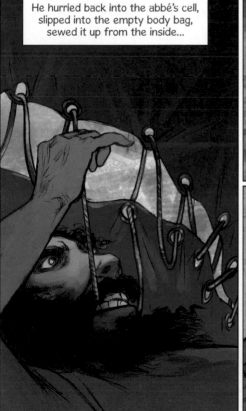

...and waited...

Best to get rid of him before morning.

We'll attach the weights to his ankles and toss him over the wall. He'll be at the bottom of the sea by daybreak.

THE SEA!

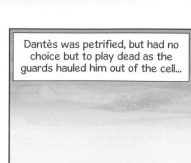

Dantès was petrified, but had no choice but to play dead as the guards hauled him out of the cell...

...up the steep cliffs...

...and into the sea!

Dantès fought against the wild current as he struggled to free himself from his bonds.

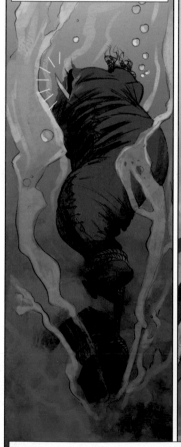

With great effort, he tore free of the sack with the help of a knife that he had hidden in his clothes and kicked off the chains. Desperately he swam up for air...

He broke the surface exhausted. Behind him was the eerie silhouette of the Château d'If, and dead ahead an island just visible at dawn.

To succumb to fatigue now when I am at the threshold of freedom would be too cruel a fate!

HUFF HUFF

HUFF HUFF

And so he summoned the last of his waning strength and began to swim.

HUFF HUFF

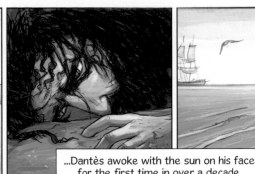

...Dantès awoke with the sun on his face for the first time in over a decade.

Free at last...

On the horizon loomed the Château d'If – his home for fourteen years and the final resting place of Abbé Faria.

Goodbye, old friend.

Knowing that the stretch of water that ran past the Château d'If was a popular trading route, Dantès tried to catch the attention of a passing ship.

His ingenuity was rewarded when a smugglers' barge spotted his signal and came to the shore.

I am stranded – the victim of a shipwreck.

I would be most grateful if you could find a post for me onboard. I am an able sailor and ask for nothing but work.

The ship's captain, a man named Jacopo, was moved by Dantès's plea and gave him work. The crew never doubted Dantès's story – he was indeed a fine seaman and earned their respect and friendship over time.

For almost a year, Dantès sailed with the smugglers, happy to be free, until one day, the ship docked for repairs at a small, deserted island...

...the Island of Monte Cristo!

Jacopo! How long will we be staying here?

Just long enough to fix the rigging. We'll set sail before sunset.

Ah, time enough for a spot of hunting, then!

Be careful, my friend. This island is treacherous.

Promising Jacopo to return on time, Dantès set off with no intention of hunting anything but the treasure.

He followed Abbé Faria's directions till he came to a wall of rock.

Hmm... this will take more time than I thought.

Ever resourceful, Dantès found a couple of fallen branches and used them as crutches on his return to the ship.

Sorry, Captain. It's my leg – I will be useless aboard. Leave me here on this island to rest and come back for me later.

Goodness! What happened to you? I told you to be careful!

Well, alright.

As soon as the ship was out of sight, Dantès cast away his fake crutches and ran back to the wall of rock.

With gunpowder stolen from the ship, he fashioned a crude bomb.

This should do the trick.

BOOM

A tunnel!

It goes on and on, down and down... this could be the place!

When Jacopo and his crew returned to Monte Cristo for Dantès, they found him in high spirits.

Edmond, my friend! Are you ready to set sail again?

Yes! Can't wait to get started!

Dantès had made sure to hide the treasure well, and took with him only what he needed to buy a new yacht with the capacity to hold the rest of his hoard.

He travelled with the sailors to Genoa where he commissioned the construction of a yacht.

I am wealthy now, Jacopo. I have come by a substantial inheritance.

Jacopo accepted Dantès's tale as the time spent with Abbé Faria had refined Dantès's manners to appear as those of a nobleman.

Dantès sent Jacopo to Marseilles to discover happy news of the loved ones he had left behind.

Go, my friend, and find out all you can about them. Meet me with the news at Monte Cristo.

But Jacopo returned to the island with nothing but report of tragedy and sadness.

What! My father dead! And no trace of Mercédès?!

No good news of Monsieur Morrel as well. He is on the verge of bankruptcy.

43

As if spurred by the unfortunate tidings, Dantès immediately set sail for Marseilles.

He was armed with an inexhaustible supply of funds and a lust for revenge.

Jacopo accompanied him as his aide, ever faithful and ready to do his bidding.

Upon arriving in Marseilles, Dantès found that money could buy just about anything, and with a few coins in the right pockets, he tracked Caderousse to the town of Beaucaire.

Disguised as Abbé Busoni, a character of his own invention, Dantès headed to a dilapidated bar, where he knew he would find his old acquaintance.

Gaspard Caderousse?

Yes... to whom am I speaking?

Abbé Busoni. And I come to you on behalf of an old friend, Edmond Dantès.

Dantès! But it has been years! Has he been freed? Is he prosperous?

I'm afraid he died a wretched, heartbroken prisoner.

How terrible! He was a good man.

Dantès never knew *why* he was imprisoned. His final wish was that I get to the bottom of the mystery.

While incarcerated, he befriended a wealthy Englishman who gave him a diamond worth 50,000 francs. Dantès requested I sell the diamond and split the profit between his friends.

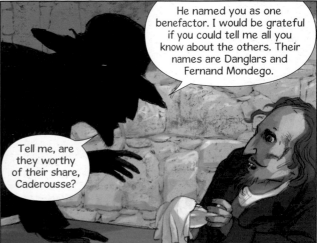

He named you as one benefactor. I would be grateful if you could tell me all you know about the others. Their names are Danglars and Fernand Mondego.

Tell me, are they worthy of their share, Caderousse?

Disguised as a financial clerk of the firm of Thomson & French, Dantès visited Monsieur de Boville, who was not only Morrel's chief creditor, but also the registrar of prisons.

Good afternoon, monsieur. I am the chief clerk of the house of Thomson & French of Rome. I was wondering if we could talk.

Well alright. Do come in.

I would like to get some information about Morrel & Son of Marseilles. Our firm has loaned quite a bit of money on their securities, and we are a little uneasy at reports that the firm is on the brink of ruin.

Monseiur Morrel is honourable to the core, but almost bankrupt and owes me 200,000 francs.

I need the money. My daughter is getting married, and I had reserved the amount for her wedding.

I will pay his total debt in cash, on one condition.

Anything!

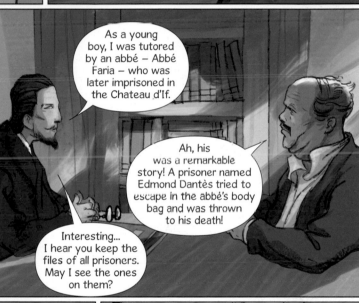

As a young boy, I was tutored by an abbé – Abbé Faria – who was later imprisoned in the Chateau d'If.

Ah, his was a remarkable story! A prisoner named Edmond Dantès tried to escape in the abbé's body bag and was thrown to his death!

Interesting... I hear you keep the files of all prisoners. May I see the ones on them?

Glad to have his money back, Monsieur de Boville handed over the files to Dantès.

I will go and put the money in my safe.

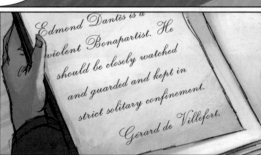

Edmond Dantès is a violent Bonapartist. He should be closely watched and guarded and kept in strict solitary confinement.

Gérard de Villefort.

47

Dantès left Monsieur de Boville's house, armed with the knowledge that Villefort was equally to blame for his imprisonment. He went straight to Morrel & Son, still disguised as the clerk of Thomson & French.

Morrel's daughter, Julie, answered the door.

Hello, may I speak with your father? I represent the house of Thomson & French, which holds the debts of Morrel & Son.

Yes, of course.

Julie showed Dantès into her father's office.

My daughter says your company holds debts of mine?

We do now, sir. We have bought the total amount of your credit, so now you are indebted to us and us alone.

Why has your company risked so much on me? Haven't you heard we have lost five ships this year? If the *Pharaon*, too, has sunk, I will be ruined.

And my poor daughter... she wishes to marry Emmanuel, her sweetheart, but I cannot afford the dowry! Life is cruel!

My employers believe you are overdue for a stroke of good fortune.

The house of Morrel & Son is a respected one, and it would be a tragedy to let it go under. You have three months to get the money, and then I will return.

If I hear you right--

Thump Thump

Just then, a group of sailors burst through the door despite Julie's attempts to stop them.

Wait, you can't go in there!

But time passed, and Morrel was unable to raise the money.

He sold everything he had to pay the wages of his loyal seamen, and his staff offered to work for free to support their honest employer, but it was not enough.

His son, Maximilien, who had been serving in the army, returned to Marseilles to help his father, but found him in an awful state.

You must hold on, Father... something will turn up!

It is over, my son. I cannot have our family name dishonoured. Leave me. Leave me now!

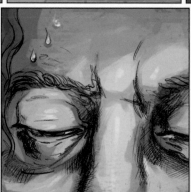

The old man could not allow the debts to go unpaid and keep living in shame.

He saw only one option.

Stop, Father!

You are saved!

Julie!

Saved? What do you mean?

Your bills have been paid! And I have been sent this diamond as a dowry. Oh, an angel has blessed us, Father! We are saved!

Emmanuel, too, arrived in a state of extreme excitement.

The *Pharaon*!? But she sank!

Monsieur, you must come at once! The *Pharaon* is coming into port!

Then she must have risen from the depths laden with cargo! A miracle, sir!

CLUNK!

Monsieur Morrel, Maximilien, Julie, and Emmanuel rushed down to the port where they were confronted by a glorious sight.

Oh, a gift from heaven it must be! It is indeed the *Pharaon*... and my old crew on board! Oh, happy day! Who have I to thank for this fortune?

At a distance, away from the crowd, a man watched the joyous scene.

Be happy, noble soul! Be blessed for all the good you have done and will do hereafter, and may my gratitude remain in obscurity as have your good deeds.

And now I must go... farewell to kindness, humanity, and gratitude. I have saved the good, and now I must punish the wicked.

PHARAON

With this firm purpose, Dantès set sail with Jacopo, leaving Marseilles behind. Morrel's honour had been restored by Dantès's generosity, and his happiness made complete by the marriage of Julie and Emmanuel.

In need of a base, Dantès returned to the Island of Monte Cristo, using his immense fortune to purchase the title of Count from the Tuscan government.

Under his new name, he existed in obscurity for the next nine years, refining his skills. His quest for vengeance took him to all corners of the globe in search of people who might aid the destruction of his enemies.

Suspicious of Fernand's military successes, Dantès headed to Greece where his rival had made most of his money. Dantès's search for the truth led him to Athens, and a young woman named Haidée.

You say you know Fernand Mondego?

Know him? That man ruined my life! He was a soldier in the French army, assigned to protect my father, the eminent Ali Pasha, from the invading Turks.

My father trusted Fernand with the care of our family, but Mondego betrayed him to the enemy and sold me and my mother into slavery! My father was murdered because of him! I would do anything to see him brought to justice.

Dantès bought Haidée from her owner, and they left Athens together.

Not only is she incredibly beautiful and a good and loyal person, Fernand's treachery towards her famous family could prove invaluable to his downfall.

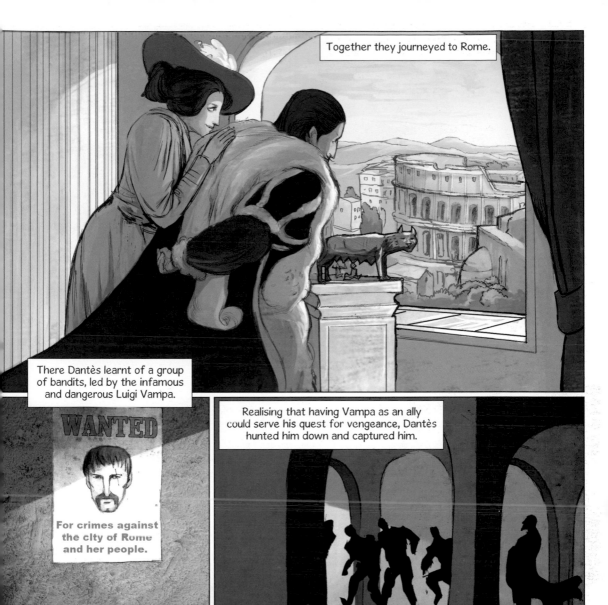

Together they journeyed to Rome.

There Dantès learnt of a group of bandits, led by the infamous and dangerous Luigi Vampa.

WANTED

For crimes against the city of Rome and her people.

Realising that having Vampa as an ally could serve his quest for vengeance, Dantès hunted him down and captured him.

Trapped and defeated, Vampa expected Dantès to turn him over to the authorities and claim the handsome reward offered for his head. But Dantès struck a deal with the feared outlaw instead.

Promise to be there when I need your help, and you will be suitably compensated.

You have my word.

Back in Marseilles, Dantès kept his ear close to the ground for any news relating to his foes.

Not long after giving Caderousse the diamond, Dantès heard that a man named Bertuccio had been imprisoned for the murder of a jeweller in possession of the very same stone.

Dantès visited Bertuccio in prison in the guise of Abbé Busoni.

You are accused of murder and theft... are you guilty?

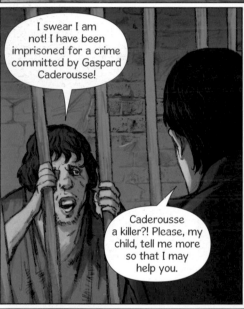

I swear I am not! I have been imprisoned for a crime committed by Gaspard Caderousse!

Caderousse a killer?! Please, my child, tell me more so that I may help you.

I'm a smuggler by trade and used to hide out at Caderousse's bar. I was there the day you gave him the diamond and followed him when he went to sell it.

And sell it he did! But his greed was too great. As soon as the money changed hands, he stabbed the buyer, and took the stone back from him!

I saw it all, and was found by the police at the site of the murder before I could flee.

57

'What became of the child?'

'Well, I could not leave the poor thing there, so I dug him up and made off into the night. I raised him myself with the help of my sister. I named him Benedetto.'

Who was the boy?

He was the illegitimate son of Villefort and his mistress!

I don't believe an honest man should be locked up, my dear Bertuccio. I will see to it that you are freed, and Caderousse punished in your place.

You are too kind, abbé. But nothing much awaits me outside these walls. Benedetto, my dear boy, has left me and fallen into a life of serious crime.

There is no one waiting for me, and nothing for me to do. It is better I serve my time in jail.

Nonsense! I have dealings with the Count of Monte Cristo, and he has asked me to find him a servant. I will recommend you for the post.

Would you? Oh, thank you, dear abbé. You are an angel amongst men!

Dantès left the prison in high spirits and immediately began searching for Benedetto.

Villefort has an illegitimate son whom he tried to kill! This is surely a secret I can make use of.

As Abbé Busoni had promised, Bertuccio was released into the service of the Count of Monte Cristo, and Caderousse was imprisoned in his place.

But Caderousse had no intention of remaining in custody, and a few years later, escaped.

He tracked down Bertuccio, who was in the count's employ, and kept a watch on him in the hope of using information about his former friend to his advantage.

But by accident, Caderousse witnessed a meeting between Benedetto and the count, and listened in as Villefort's illegitimate son struck a deal with Monte Cristo.

Your father tells me you have fallen in with some bad people, Benedetto.

A life of crime is the only life I have ever known. The police are after me.

I have a proposition for you, Benedetto – one that will help us both.

I know your *real* father is Gérard de Villefort, and I intend to destroy him.

I want you to pose as Andrea Cavalcanti, a wealthy Italian whom I will induct into Parisian society once I am established in the capital.

I will finance your transformation and keep you safe until the time is right for your arrest. At the trial, you must follow my instructions, and then I will see you freed. What do you say?

It's a deal!

With this information, I can blackmail Benedetto! He will surely pay to keep his true identity a secret.

With a global network of allies in place, Dantès, now under the permanent guise of the Count of Monte Cristo, travelled to Rome in pursuit of Albert de Morcerf – son of Fernand and Mercédès.

He checked in to the same hotel as Albert and his friend, Baron Franz d'Épinay, and booked the room next to theirs.

Rome was then buzzing in anticipation of a carnival due to be held that weekend.

The streets were packed, and all the seats for the carnival had already been sold.

The only way left to watch the procession was from a coach, the price of which had trebled for the occasion.

The Count of Monte Cristo had a plan.

Good afternoon, sir. I have a message for Albert de Morcerf from the Count of Monte Cristo.

I am Albert. What does the illustrious count say?

He was wondering if you and your friend would join him in his private coach for the carnival this weekend. He would be most honoured.

The honour would be ours! We accept!

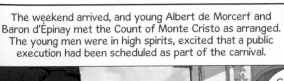

The weekend arrived, and young Albert de Morcerf and Baron d'Épinay met the Count of Monte Cristo as arranged. The young men were in high spirits, excited that a public execution had been scheduled as part of the carnival.

Good morning, gentlemen. How are you both today?

We are most grateful, sir. Your generosity has afforded us a fine view! Franz and I are eager to see the hanging!

Entertaining as it is, my young friends, I have always found execution an unsatisfactory mode of punishment.

It is over far too quickly. Those who have caused suffering, should be made to suffer in turn.

An interesting view, dear count, but no reason to miss the event! Drive on!

Hurrah!

The unlikely trio reached the site of the execution.

Where is he going?

That woman in the crowd was waving at him. I think he has gone to try his luck! He is always up to no good.

I say, that woman just asked me to meet her tomorrow morning! What a fine day I'm having! And it's all thanks to our host, the Count of Monte Cristo.

The next morning, Franz woke up to find Albert's bed empty.

I don't know where Albert arranged to meet that mysterious woman. Maybe the count will know.

Good morning, Franz. I was expecting you.

Expecting me? Why?

Albert has been kidnapped.

By the woman?!

No, she was a decoy to lure him away from our protection. I found a note waiting for me when I got up. It is from Luigi Vampa.

That notorious bandit? What does he want from you?

Money. Vampa is demanding a ransom for Albert's safe return.

We must go to his aid, Franz. He needs us.

Well done Luigi, my friend, for carrying out my plan so perfectly. I now have Albert in the palm of my hand!

62

With impressive authority and a seeming disregard for his own safety, the Count of Monte Cristo ordered Bertuccio to ready the coach. And they went off in pursuit of Vampa without further delay.

Drive like the wind, Bertuccio...

...we cannot afford to waste a single minute.

By midday, they had found and caught up with the bandits.

Vampa! What do you mean by kidnapping my friend?

I mean to make money, Monte Cristo. Perhaps we should talk this over in private?

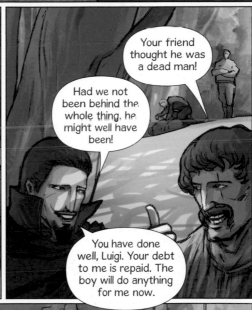

Your friend thought he was a dead man!

Had we not been behind the whole thing, he might well have been!

You have done well, Luigi. Your debt to me is repaid. The boy will do anything for me now.

I have negotiated the terms of your release, Albert. Let us go, gentlemen.

Albert, the count has saved your life!

True. Dearest count, I owe you my life. Ask of me anything, and I will not refuse.

I wish for nothing more than to be introduced to your friends and family in Paris. I will call on you in three months' time to arrange things.

Three months later, Albert invited the count to his family home in Paris. He had asked his friends Baron Château-Renaud and Maximilien Morrel to attend, in the hope that they could introduce the count to the people he wished to meet.

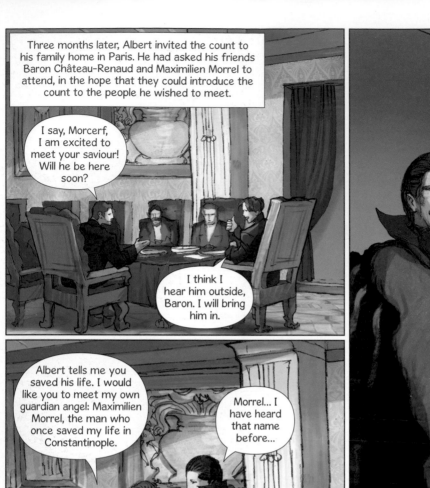

I say, Morcerf, I am excited to meet your saviour! Will he be here soon?

I think I hear him outside, Baron. I will bring him in.

Albert tells me you saved his life. I would like you to meet my own guardian angel: Maximilien Morrel, the man who once saved my life in Constantinople.

Morrel... I have heard that name before...

Gentlemen, may I present the Count of Monte Cristo!

Yes sir, my father owns a shipping company that was in the news some time ago.

We were on the brink of financial ruin, but were saved by the generosity of a mysterious benefactor.

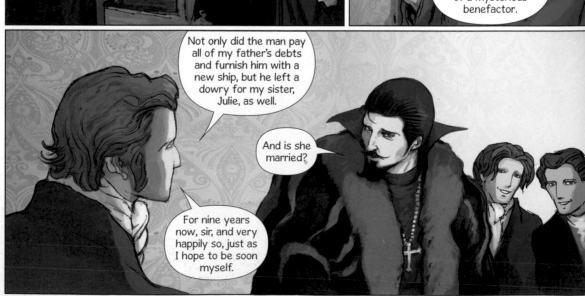

Not only did the man pay all of my father's debts and furnish him with a new ship, but he left a dowry for my sister, Julie, as well.

And is she married?

For nine years now, sir, and very happily so, just as I hope to be soon myself.

I am very happy for you and your family, Maximilien. I hope to see a lot more of you now that I have moved to Paris.

Oh, you have moved here? If you need anything, I would be happy to be of help! Where are you staying?

I have bought a property on the Champs-Élysées and another in Auteuil – No. 28, Rue de la Fontaine. You should visit me sometime, Maximilien. I believe we will become the best of friends.

I am honoured that you should say so, sir – of course I shall visit soon!

I think you will fit in very well in Paris, Monte Cristo. You already look the part! So elegant! Tell me, what is the story behind your emerald pill box?

It is one of three such stones. I used one of its brothers to free a woman and the other to save a man's life. I had this one hollowed out to carry my hashish pills.

Treasure has no value unless it can be used for good.

At that moment, Fernand Mondego, the Comte de Morcerf, entered the room.

Father! I'd like you to meet my friend, the Count of Monte Cristo.

It's a pleasure!

Indeed it is...

Why don't you and I take a drink together, Count? I would very much like to thank you privately for saving my son's life.

Are you enjoying Paris?

Very much so. I am eternally grateful to your son for agreeing to introduce me to the city and her people.

But it is I who am grateful to you, Count. You saved my son's life. For that I am forever in your debt. Is there anything I can do to repay you?

Well... I am keen to mingle with the Parisian elite. I am accustomed to people of influence, you see.

Why, I have a fantastic idea! My good friend Danglars is a member of the Chamber of Commerce! He is a man of money and power and would be honoured to receive you!

Danglars! At last!

That would be perfect. I look forward to meeting him.

Ah, here comes my beautiful wife!

Mercédès!

Edmond!

Oh, goodness... I...

She has recognised me!

Darling! Are you okay?

Albert! Fetch your mother a glass of water.

Here you go, Mother. Drink this.

Oh Edmond, dear, sweet Edmond. What is it you want? Your disguise terrifies me: why do you hide behind this mask unless your intentions are evil?

Do you feel better, Mother?

Yes, yes, I feel quite well now.

Albert, don't trust the Count of Monte Cristo. He seems a great man, but could be capable of anything. Be on your guard!

It was not long before the count and Fernand went to meet Danglars at the Chamber of Commerce where they were told he was working from home.

Monsieur, if you could put in a word about me to Monsieur Danglars, I could visit him in private. I wish to discuss business with him.

I will do that, Monte Cristo.

A few days later, with Jacopo in tow, the count headed to Danglars's address.

Monte Cristo, I presume?

Monsieur Danglars. A pleasure to meet you. I am new to Paris, and my friend, Fernand Mondego, has advised me that you are the person to introduce me to the right kind of people in this city.

Friend of Fernand or not, why should I help you?

I will offer you unlimited credit with my firm, the house of Thomson & French, and will lend you the services of Jacopo, my financial advisor, should you agree to be my social guide.

Unless you cannot handle credit?

My vast fortune can cover any debt! It is a deal.

Good. I should return home now, but Jacopo will be with you for a while and explain the details.

Please take my wife's carriage. She is about to return from the opera with her friend, Madame de Villefort.

Pleased that Danglars had been arrogant enough to accept his offer of unlimited credit, Dantès met Madame Danglars's coach as it pulled up.

Whoa, there!

There, there. Calm down.

Good evening, sir.

Good evening to you, Madame Danglars.

Gérard de Villefort's beautiful and young second wife was in the carriage with her son, Édouard.

You are very good with animals, Monsieur...

Monte Cristo... the *Count* of Monte Cristo. And you are Madame de Villefort, are you not?

Indeed I am.

Monsieur Danglars insisted that I ride with you. Do you mind?

Not in the slightest, dear sir!

The phial of elixir brought young Édouard back to consciousness at once.

Dantès returned to his Champs-Élysées home, where he found Haidée waiting for him.

Good evening, Count. Did Danglars fall for your trick?

Yes, he has accepted more credit than he can afford to manage. With Jacopo's ill advice, he will lose everything. It is only a matter of time.

I want to release you, Haidée. You are a fine and noble woman and don't deserve the life or title of a slave. You are free to do as you wish.

But promise me, you will not reveal your identity to anyone.

That I promise, but I will not leave. I will remain in Paris, in hiding, so that I am not spotted by Fernand. I will be here for you whenever you need me.

Sweet Haidée, I knew I could rely on you. I need you now more than ever, and your integrity has made it possible for you to help me as a free woman. I am truly blessed.

The count arose early the next morning to find a letter waiting for him.

From Gérard de Villefort, thanking me for my chivalry.

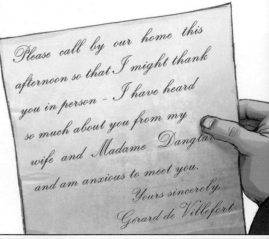

Please call by our home this afternoon so that I might thank you in person – I have heard so much about you from my wife and Madame Danglar and am anxious to meet you.

Yours sincerely,
Gérard de Villefort

Not one to pass up an opportunity to stand face to face with the enemy, Dantès set off for Villefort's home at once.

So nice of you to come, Count! Perhaps you can share with me your knowledge of potions before my husband is ready to receive you.

Exactly which field are you interested in, Madame? There is so much to know!

Poisons. Many men wish my husband dead. I want to recognise and understand poisons in case...

...an attempt should be made on his life.

She is lying – there is evil in her eyes. If I teach her all I know about poisons, she will no doubt use it to kill. Still, she may aid my cause, so I will help her.

72

After the shocking revelation, the party was alive with whispered gossip, till the time came for the guests to leave. Villefort hurried away, observed closely by Andrea Cavalcanti...

...but when Andrea entered the carriage...

Hello, Benedetto.

Caderousse! What are you doing here, you worm?

Life on the run is hard; I need more money. And I know how much you value your new identity.

So, if you want to keep it a secret, hand over your diamond ring and tell me how to break in to Monte Cristo's Champs-Élysées home. I have seen you watching the place!

If you want to rob the count, you should know he *always* leaves his windows open at night. But I warn you, he is a dangerous man. Goodbye, Caderousse.

The Count of Monte Cristo bade farewell to the last of his guests, and was about to retire when...

KNOCK KNOCK

Danglars! To what do I owe this pleasure?

Bad news, Monte Cristo, very bad news! Jacopo advised that I sell my Spanish shares due to political unrest in the country. I did as he said, and I have lost 700,000 francs!

But Danglars, you assured me your *vast* fortune could cover any extension I offered!

The fool is too arrogant to admit he cannot afford to pay.

I have an idea, Danglars. I hear your daughter Eugénie is engaged to Albert de Morcerf... am I correct?

You are, but how do you know?

I have my sources... Why not revoke the engagement and pledge her to Andrea Cavalcanti instead.

I hear he is looking for a Parisian bride, and he most certainly has the funds to get you out of this mess.

I am sure he does, but would he lend me the money?

For your daughter's hand in marriage? Undoubtedly! Now go home to bed. I will see that the arrangements are made.

Dantès's plan was working perfectly. He had effectively removed yet another lifeline – the Morcerf family fortune – to which Danglars might have been able to cling.

76

Meanwhile at the Villefort residence, Gérard de Villefort was agonising over the count's revelation.

How can he possibly know *everything*... I *know* there was not a body in that garden when I searched for it. So he *must* know the truth.

Why else would he bring me there and put on that show, unless he *wanted* me to know that he knows my secret.

There is more to this Count of Monte Cristo than meets the eye. I will find out who he *really* is by the end of the week... even if it kills me!

Gérard! My husband is dead, and I fear I will not last much longer. I have been feeling unwell for days – there is murder in the air!

The interruption came from Marquise de Saint-Méran, the mother of Villefort's first wife, Renée.

What would you have me do, Marquise? Assign guards to your chambers? This is your home! Who would want to kill you?

I don't know, Gérard, but I suspect foul play. I want you to bring forward Valentine's wedding. I want to see her married before I die.

You are in no danger, Marquise. But I will do as you ask. The wedding will be within the month.

It cannot be... I love Maximilien, not Franz!

Distraught at what she had heard, Valentine fled to the attic where the family kept Noirtier, her grandfather, hidden away.

Noirtier had once been a proud man, but his body was now ravaged with age and illness. His mind, however, was still as sharp as a knife and his heart as soft as a cloud.

Grandfather... I need your help. Father is going to make me marry Franz d'Épinay, but I am in love with Maximilien Morrel!

Although he struggled to communicate with most, Valentine had learnt to understand her ailing grandfather's cracked speech as if he were talking freely.

I can get rid of Baron d'Épinay if you bring him to me. But what about Maximilien? Where is he now?

He is on his way here now. I am supposed to meet him at the gate but... my goodness, I am late already!

Maximilien? What--

Valentine, my love, I have just heard something terrible!

I grew tired of waiting for you outside, so I climbed the gate and sneaked across the garden. I heard your father saying that your grandmother has been found dead! Poisoned!

Marquise de Saint-Méran's death confirmed her suspicion that evil was stalking the Villefort mansion. But the young lovers and their doting protector could not dwell on the tragedy. They finalised their plan and sent word for Franz to call the next day.

The next morning, Franz d'Épinay arrived at the Villefort residence, thinking he had been called to discuss details of the wedding. He was greeted by Barrois, Noirtier's manservant.

Good morning, Baron. My master would like to speak to you.

Your master? Why on earth would Senator Noirtier want to see me?

Franz and Noirtier had never met, and all Franz knew about the old man was that he had known his father at the time of his mysterious death.

You wanted to see me, sir?

Before you marry my granddaughter, d'Épinay, I think you should read this.

Minutes of a Bonapartist meeting dated 15th February 1815, the day your father was killed.

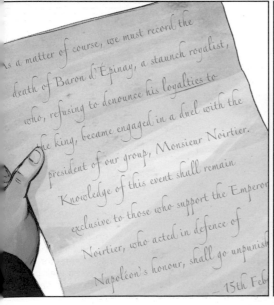

As a matter of course, we must record the death of Baron d'Épinay, a staunch royalist, who, refusing to denounce his loyalties to the king, became engaged in a duel with the president of our group, Monsieur Noirtier. Knowledge of this event shall remain exclusive to those who support the Emperor. Noirtier, who acted in defence of Napoleon's honour, shall go unpunish[ed]

— 15th Feb

You killed my father!? I will NEVER marry into a family that harbours a murderer. The wedding is off!

And with that, Franz stormed out, never to return.

79

Valentine and Maximilien, who had been hiding in the shadows, rejoined Noirtier to celebrate.

Oh grandfather, you did it! I am free to marry my love!

I don't know how to thank you, monsieur.

Just be happy together...

Wise words, master! Now let us raise a toast to the happy couple! To Valentine and Maximilien!

Gaa! I can't breathe... everything is... going... black...

POISON!

The count heard of Barrois's death the next day, and resolved to do what he could to protect Valentine from the serial killer – the identity of whom he was sure he knew.

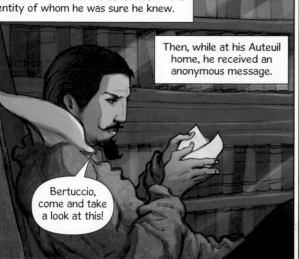

Then, while at his Auteuil home, he received an anonymous message.

Bertuccio, come and take a look at this!

Your Champs-Élysées home will be robbed tonight by Gaspard Caderousse.

This is Benedetto's handwriting!

Caderousse must be following him, or else he would have told me about this personally.

Bertuccio, have all my Champs-Élysées staff take the night off. I will deal with this... personally.

Dantès set off across town, disguised as Abbé Busoni. By the time he reached his Champs-Élysées apartment, night had fallen.

Caderousse!

Ah, and there is Cavalcanti! It looks like he is planning to catch Caderousse when he comes out of the building.

I will slip into the house without making contact with Cavalcanti.

I can hear Caderousse rifling through my things.

GASPARD CADEROUSSE! You have sinned!

Abbé Busoni!

Please, please, forgive me, I beg you!

You have squandered your previous chances at redemption. Why should I spare you again?

I will change, I know I can change!

Very well, I will let you leave this place. If you make it home alive, it will be a sign from God that you have been pardoned. Now get out of my sight!

Gaa!

But Cavalcanti had been waiting patiently for Caderousse to emerge from the house, and when he did, Cavalcanti moved swiftly.

84

Is he breathing?

No, sir, he is dead, but there is a statement pinned to his chest.

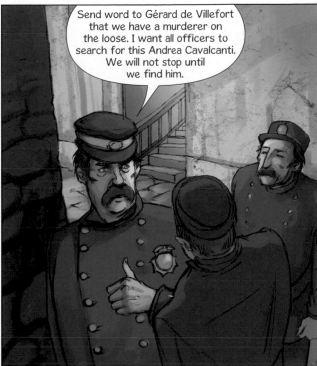

Send word to Gérard de Villefort that we have a murderer on the loose. I want all officers to search for this Andrea Cavalcanti. We will not stop until we find him.

My plan is working perfectly – helped by the police, no less. Now that Caderousse has sealed his own fate, I must turn my attentions to Fernand.

I think a little trip is in order. I should not be here when the hammer-blow is struck.

And so Dantès sent an invitation to Fernand's son, Albert de Morcerf, whose unwitting cooperation would be essential for his treacherous father's collapse.

The next morning.

It really is very nice of you to invite me to your holiday home in Normandy, Count.

It does a young man good to get out of the city once in a while, and I enjoy your company, Albert. You are, in a way, the son I never had.

Dear God, no! It cannot be!

What on earth is the matter?

We must return to Paris at once! My father is in trouble!

What a *surprise...*

At almost the same time, Fernand arrived at the Chamber of Commerce, unaware of the story printed about him in that morning's paper.

Good lord, there's an awful commotion inside... I wonder what's amiss.

This is an outrage!

Traitor!

Monster!

Disgrace!

Fernand de Morcerf, you are accused of political treachery and the abuse of your military powers for financial gain, resulting in the murder of the Greek Ali Pasha.

No... it's not true!

You have gained wealth and power by devious means; you will stand trial for the crimes charged.

I don't know what you are talking about. I am innocent. There is no proof!

We have a witness. I call to the stand Haidée, daughter of the late Ali Pasha.

This monster killed my father, stole his fortune, and sold me and my mother into slavery. He should hang for his crimes!

No, no, it can't be... I am finished.

Liar

Traitor

The people who had helped Fernand scale dizzying heights of success now collectively castigated him.

When Fernand most needed a friend, he was blessed with the sudden appearance of Albert on his way to the Chamber of Commerce.

Father!

My son! I am so glad you are here. I thought you were in Normandy!

I came back when I saw the morning paper. Father, who has done this to you? Who has betrayed our family honour?

I don't know, my son, but there is no way out of this.

It is true, then? Did anyone else know your secret?

Danglars knew, but he would not have done this.

It must be someone else... someone who has come into our lives recently... someone we know very little about...

Monte Cristo!

88

The next morning, the count, along with Maximilien Morrel and Emmanuel, arrived early at the meeting place.

Count, I am worried you underestimate Albert.

He may be young and rash, but the lad holds a pistol as well as he does a wine glass!

If you don't mind, Maximilien, would you be so kind as to place these four playing cards in the corners of this frame and place it thirty yards away?

Of course.

I hope you have got a few tricks left up your sleeve, Monte Cristo.

I won't be needing any tricks, my friend. Watch this.

BANG

BANG

BANG

BANG

That was amazing! I have no doubt you will win!

There was never any doubt in my mind that I could kill young Albert, but I'm afraid that he will kill me. I have promised an old friend that I will lose. Call it a matter of honour...

NO!

NO!

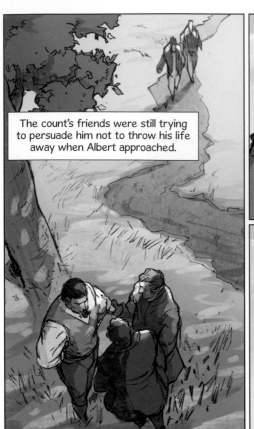

The count's friends were still trying to persuade him not to throw his life away when Albert approached.

You have come then...

...to restore my family's honour.

My mother told me everything... who you are... what my father did to you... how you promised to let me live...

There will be no killing today. Forgive me, Count, you are no enemy of mine.

Albert left Monte Cristo and returned home at once to pack his things.

I can no longer stay in Paris, under the cloud of my father's shame.

I am leaving, Mother. I have come to say goodbye.

Where will you go, my son?

Far away from here... from him... I will go somewhere where I can make a name for myself.

And so you shall, my son – a name free of disgrace and full of honour.

Excuse me, madame, but a message has arrived for you.

It is from Edmond!

Dearest Mercédès,
I have buried 3,000 francs in the garden of my father's home—the home that was to be our first together. It is yours. Please take it and start a life away from Fernand.
Yours always,
Edmond.

He is a fine man, this Edmond Dantès...

The finest... I will do as he says and take the money to a convent where I will live out my remaining days. Goodbye, dear son, live well!

Meanwhile, the count and Maximilien were on their way home.

Can I offer you breakfast, Maximilien?

I would love to, Count, but I am anxious to see Valentine.

Ah, your sweetheart, of course. Well, let me not keep you. I know what it is like to be young and in love.

Ah, to be in love...

I had almost forgotten the feeling in that dark, dank cell, but there is a woman whose strength and beauty has reminded me... Haidée...

What are you doing alive, Monte Cristo!? I demand to know why my son *apologised* to you rather than shoot you down like the dog that you are!

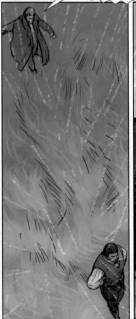

Your son is a man of honour. He admitted his mistake before tarnishing your family name further.

You lie! You tricked him like you tricked everyone else. If he won't kill you, then I will. I insist we duel instead.

Disguised again as the Count of Monte Cristo, Dantès dashed to Danglars's house where the marriage contract between his daughter Eugénie and the fugitive Andrea Cavalcanti was about to be signed.

Monte Cristo! Glad you could make it. Come in...

Madame de Villefort had been asked to come, and along with Monte Cristo, was to act as witness to the ceremony.

I wonder where my husband is. I haven't seen him all day!

I'm afraid I may be responsible for his absence. He is inquiring into a robbery and murder at my Champs-Élysées home. The thief was called Caderousse, and his murderer is still at large.

This is awful! Caderousse is dead and Fernand ruined by this morning's paper... is fate catching up with us?

I see...

KNOCK KNOCK

Afternoon, sir, sorry to disturb you, but we have reason to believe you are harbouring a fugitive.

A fugitive!

Yes sir, he goes by the name of Andrea Cavalcanti but is an imposter whose real name is Benedetto. He is wanted for the killing of Gaspard Caderousse.

But... but...

Gentlemen, you are too late! Benedetto was here, but he seems to have disappeared. If you hurry, you might catch him!

!!?

Thank goodness I don't have to marry that awful man! I will never forgive you for this, Father. I am leaving and will never come back!

No! I need Cavalcanti's funds to pay off my debts to Monte Cristo's firm! This is bad... very bad indeed...

Does anyone know where the fugitive has gone?

If he can avoid the streets, he will avoid your gaze. Tell your men to turn their eyes skywards in their search.

Travelling by coach, it did not take the police long to catch up with Benedetto, who was fleeing over the rooftops.

Benedetto moved lithely like a cat...

...but was hopelessly outnumbered.

He had to leave the rooftops eventually...

...and when he did, the police were on the ground waiting for him.

It's over, Benedetto!

That night, Dantès, disguised as Abbé Busoni, sneaked into Valentine de Villefort's bedroom through the open window...

ABBÉ!

Shush, child. I am here to help you. You must listen very carefully and do as I say, or in the morning you will be dead.

The young woman had, upon her father's advice, taken Busoni into her confidence and trusted the wise abbé.

Your stepmother, Madame de Villefort, is trying to poison you.

She has already killed your mother's parents and tried to kill Noirtier too. She wants your inheritance for her own son, Édouard.

Next to your bed is a glass of water laced with poison. If you drink it, you will die. Drink this instead, it will put you to sleep. But you must trust me.

I do trust you, dear abbé. I will do as you say.

The next morning, Villefort went to his daughter's bedroom.

Valentine? Darling, are you alright?

There was no answer. Terrified, Villefort burst into the room.

What awaited him was a horrifying sight...

Valentine was cold as ice and not breathing...

She is dead! My darling daughter is dead!

What is going on?

Maximilien... Father... Valentine is dead!

Dead? But how!?

Poison! Just like the Saint-Mérans... like Barrois... I want you both to keep this to yourselves.

I will find out who is responsible and deal with them myself.

Are you alright, monsieur? I was passing by and heard a shout!

My dear abbé, Valentine is dead! I should arrange her funeral, but I must attend to the Cavalcanti case. Could you take care of it for me?

Of course. Leave me here with her and attend to your business.

How can he think of work at a time like this? The woman I love is dead, and I have nothing left to live for.

I will be with you soon, my love, I promise you that.

Grieve not, Noirtier. Your granddaughter is alive and merely sleeping. We will take her to the attic. Keep her safe and keep this to yourself. Trust me.

If what you say is true, Abbé, I might start believing in your God... but you must tell me everything.

...so those are the details of my plan. Guard your granddaughter – I must now go and find Maximilien before it is too late.

Maximilien! WAIT!

What more is there to wait for? The woman I love – the woman I had been waiting to marry – is dead! My mind is made up, Abbé. I am going to end my misery.

You cannot, Maximilien! You must think of your family, think of your dear father!

What do you know of my father? You are a good man, Abbé, but you hardly know me!

That is not true. We know each other better than you realise... I am not an abbé at all. You know me as the Count of Monte Cristo, but my real name is Edmond Dantès.

Dantès? My father's friend? But he is dead!

No, I survived the Château d'If and escaped. It was I who saved your family's honour in Marseilles; I who provided Julie's dowry; I who rebuilt the *Pharaon* and paid your father's debts.

Don't take your life, Maximilien. You must trust me. I will make everything alright.

I... I will do as you say...

Maximilien returned home to think over the exceptional turn of events. And Dantès – dressed as the count – went to Danglars's house with a plan in mind.

KNOCK KNOCK

Monte Cristo! What do you want?

It is time for you to pay your debt to my company. Jacopo tells me you now owe *five million* francs. I want it in bank notes by midnight. You know where to find me.

Dantès didn't hang around to negotiate, and left Danglars to sweat...

I can't afford to pay... I'm broke!

That snake Jacopo fed me bad advice...

But there is hope!

Danglars sped to Rome, the headquarters of Thomson & French, intending to withdraw more money and go into hiding, before they received the message to suspend his credit.

But Dantès had predicted his enemy's move, and had already sent Jacopo to Rome to enlist the help of Luigi Vampa and his bandits.

Meanwhile, Gérard de Villefort was sitting alone in his study.

I know it to be true... I wish I was wrong but it is as clear as day...

What is wrong, my love?

What is wrong? I will tell you: my daughter is dead...

...and I know who killed her.

Who?

My own wife!

No!

You have two choices...

Either you die by public execution, or by some of the poison you used on others! I will leave it up to you to decide, but when I return from the trial of Cavalcanti, I do not want to see you alive!

Villefort left for the court house a broken man.

103

As the prosecutor approached the building, Bertuccio slipped inside and searched for his son.

My boy!

Father! What are you doing here?

Come closer, I have a message for you from the Count of Monte Cristo...

As the guards approached to take their prisoner...

...Bertuccio hid in the shadows.

Time to go, Cavalcanti.

Good luck, my boy, have courage!

Cavalcanti was led to the dock. He stood in silence with a look of calm on his face.

MURDERER!

FRAUD!

Andrea Cavalcanti, you are accused of murdering the thief Gaspard Caderousse and avoiding arrest. How do you plead?

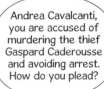

Oh, to those charges I plead guilty, but there is one error in your accusation... the name under which I am being tried.

You know me as Andrea Cavalcanti or Benedetto, but neither is my birth name.

GASP!

OH!

I am the illegitimate son of Gérard de Villefort, and I demand to stand trial under the name of my father, who buried me alive when I was an infant!

Suddenly the crowd's anger was directed away from Cavalcanti and focussed on Villefort. The prosecutor shrank back in his chair, defeated.

Liar!

Cheat!

MURDERER!

I cannot hide anymore... I am finished.

The next day, Dantès and Bertuccio set sail for Rome in pursuit of Danglars.

Are you alright, sir? You look lost in thought.

I am wondering if I have gone too far, Bertuccio. My revenge claimed the life of an innocent child. I never intended for Édouard de Villefort to die.

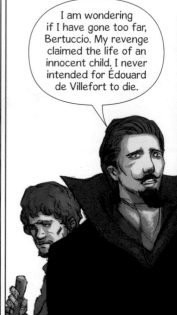

I had planned his father's downfall to the last detail, but I could not anticipate the extent of his mother's evil.

But gazing upon my old home reminds me of my quest.

I am a servant of providence, and it is my duty to deliver punishment to those who do wrong. If the hands of fate see it fit to snatch away the life of an innocent, then so be it!

I, too, was innocent once...

The count arrived in Rome and met up with Luigi Vampa.

Do you have Danglars?

Yes, we caught him as soon as he arrived. Quite an arrogant man.

At first he was sure of release, but since then... well, we have broken his spirit.

I knew I could count on you, Luigi. What have you done to him?

We have been charging him 100,000 francs for every item of food he consumes. He has only been with us a week but has aged many years. Come, see for yourself...

The final act of revenge was close... Dantès could feel it...

Prisoner! Have you suffered?

There are others who have suffered more than I, but they were martyrs...

Do you repent for your sins, Danglars? Do you repent?

I do, oh I do. But whose voice is this that addresses me? That of an angel or a devil?

A fortnight later, Dantès was waiting on the Island of Monte Cristo for the arrival of his friend, Maximilien Morrel.

With two of his four betrayers dead, one insane, and the other a ruined man, Dantès had one final mission to complete...

I have come as requested, Dantès. I have put off taking my life until now, as a favour to you. Now tell me, why have you brought me here?

It is as good a place as any! In my experience, the weather is good here and the women are second to none.

Stop playing with me, Dantès! You know I will never look at another woman; Valentine was everything to me.

Ah, Maximilien, the sun is making you crazy. Why not rest a while in the shade of that cave.

Your words make me angry, Dantès.

VALENTINE! YOU ARE ALIVE!

Well, I never! What have you found in the cave, Maximilien?

A reason to live, Dantès! You knew all along, didn't you? I am not angry, my dear friend, but tell me, why did you make me suffer so?

So that you may truly appreciate joy.

Remember this, Maximilien: All human wisdom is summed up in two words – wait and hope.

And what will become of you? Where will you go?

I have achieved what I set out to achieve, and now I plan to begin a new life with Haidée. I have told her how I feel, and she loves me too. I hope there is happiness yet for us.

Here, catch!

Keys?

To my house on the Champs-Élysées, and my holiday home in Normandy. They are my wedding gift to you. I wish you both all the happiness in the world. Live long and love each other well. Fate rewards the deserving few. Goodbye!

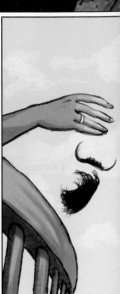

And so Edmond Dantès sailed away with his new love, Haidée. His providential mission was over: the evil had been punished and the good rewarded.

No longer the angel of destiny, Dantès was at last free to resume the life that the greed and cowardice of others had so cruelly snatched from him all those years ago.

PRISON? WHAT PRISON?

In *The Count of Monte Cristo*, Edmond Dantès manages to break out of the supposedly escape-proof island prison, the Château d'If. In reality, though, no one ever escaped that fortress-like prison. This is a fact.

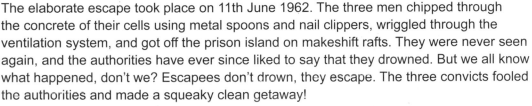

The same could be said of Alcatraz, the world's most famous island prison. Used as a setting in many books and films, Alcatraz was also known to be escape-proof. But not so for Frank Morris, and brothers John and Clarence Anglin. Before the terrible trio made the first ever escape off the island, there were 14 other attempts that ended in not so happy consequences for the escapees. So, you can imagine what was going through the heads of the three men who finally did make their way out of Alcatraz.

The elaborate escape took place on 11th June 1962. The three men chipped through the concrete of their cells using metal spoons and nail clippers, wriggled through the ventilation system, and got off the prison island on makeshift rafts. They were never seen again, and the authorities have ever since liked to say that they drowned. But we all know what happened, don't we? Escapees don't drown, they escape. The three convicts fooled the authorities and made a squeaky clean getaway!

When we talk about American high-security prisons, one image comes to our mind: lots and lots of guards and guns. So, we can assume that the seven men who escaped The John B Connally Unit maximum security prison in Texas in 2000 gargled gravel for breakfast. Dubbed the Texas Seven, the men overpowered the guards during lunchtime, when the prison is at its slowest, and stole their clothes and guns. They then proceeded to steal a police car and just drove out of the building! No one suspected a thing until the guards discovered their colleagues bound and gagged. Eventually though, six of the seven men were recaptured.

SPIES IN DISGUISE

Edmond Dantès was also a master of disguise. In *The Count of Monte Cristo*, Edmond relied on his skills of misdirection and disguise to fool all the people who wronged him and got his revenge.

History abounds in examples of such masters of disguise. Most were either soldiers or women who were thrust into war and had to use smart and tactical disguises to remain hidden and avoid getting killed. One famous master of disguise, or should we say mistress of disguise, was Sarah Emma Edmonds. Born in 1841 in Canada, Sarah was always fascinated with dressing up like a man. She would impersonate men and try to sell bibles at places where woman weren't allowed. After Abraham Lincoln was elected President of the United States in 1860, eleven southern states declared secession from the United States to form the Confederate States of America, and this was the starting point of the American Civil War. Sarah enlisted as a Confederate volunteer, but really worked as a spy for the Union Army, to avenge a friend who was executed by the Confederate troops. She assumed all manner of disguises – most famously using silver nitrate to dye her skin black to impersonate a black man! Her cover up worked so well that even the soldiers in her platoon could not tell the difference. They almost always assumed that she was a man!

THE MOON SISTERS

On the other side of the political divide, Ginnie and Lottie Moon disguised themselves as old women to spy for the Confederates during the Civil War. They transported countless bottles of morphine, pounds of opium, and endless medical supplies for wounded Confederate soldiers, all hidden in their quilted skirts!

Young d'Artagnan has only one ambition – to be a king's musketeer some day.

With these dreams, he reaches Paris. Monsieur de Treville makes him a member of the king's guards, and promises that if he proves his worth he can become a musketeer one day.

In Paris, d'Artagnan befriends the three musketeers Athos, Porthos, and Aramis, and also falls in love with the beautiful Constance Bonancieux, Queen Anne's linen maid.

But little does he know that Queen Anne would soon be in trouble with her husband, King Louise XIII, because of her secret lover, which is what the Cardinal wants. With Constance begging him to help, and the wicked Cardinal and his men chasing him, will d'Artagnan be able to save the queen's honour? Will he ever fulfil his dream of being a musketeer?

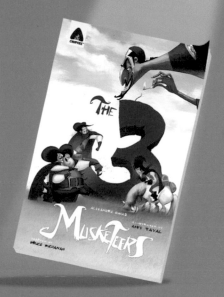

You may also like to read other titles from our

CLASSICS SERIES

TREASURE ISLAND

'Fifteen men on the dead man's chest – Yo-ho-ho, and a bottle of rum.'

Life changes for Jim Hawkins the day a mysterious sailor walks into his father's inn. The sailor possesses a secret that is in hot demand – a map which indicates the whereabouts of some hidden treasure… and people are willing to kill for it! Will Jim outwit all to recover the buried treasure? Or will he fall prey to the murderous intent of others?

THE PRISONER OF ZENDA

When Rudolf Rassendyll travels to see his distant cousin crowned king of Ruritania, it soon becomes apparent that it is not going to be a normal trip – he realises that he bears an uncanny resemblance to his cousin, and that Black Michael, a relative of the rightful king, is determined to crown himself. What follows is an adventure involving abduction, imprisonment, and deceit that will determine not only Rudolf's future, but the futures of the king, Princess Flavia, and the whole of Ruritania.

DR JEKYLL AND MR HYDE

Bold, visionary Henry Jekyll believes he can use his scientific knowledge to divide a person into two beings – one of pure good and one of pure evil. Working tirelessly in his secret laboratory, concocting a potion that would tear at the core of what makes a man human, he eventually succeeds – but only halfway. Can Jekyll undo what he has done? Or will it change things forever?

FRANKENSTEIN

Man has long had the power to take life, but what will happen when he learns to give it? Intrigued by this question, young Victor Frankenstein – a devoted student of science – becomes obsessed with the idea of conjuring life out of 'lifeless matter', and creates a being from scavenged and stolen body parts. He rejects his hideous creation, but realises he cannot escape the responsibilities of being creator, as the thing created struggles to be recognised as a thinking, feeling being.